AYLESBURY
A Pictorial History

Duck End, Aylesbury, where many of the cottagers reared Aylesbury ducks for the London market. Some of the larger houses must once have been farmhouses with barns, home closes and strips in the open fields.

AYLESBURY
A Pictorial History

Hugh Hanley
and
Julian Hunt

Phillimore

1993

Published by
PHILLIMORE & CO. LTD.
Shopwyke Manor Barn, Chichester, West Sussex
in association with
Buckinghamshire County Library

ISBN 0 85033 873 5

Printed and bound in Great Britain by
BIDDLES LTD.
Guildford, Surrey

List of Illustrations

Frontispiece: Duck End

1. Bryant's map of Buckinghamshire 1824
2. Kingsbury Square
3. Sale of the Manor of Aylesbury, 1848
4. Manor House, Bierton Hill
5. The Prebendal House
6. St Osyth's, Parson's Fee
7. Spittle Mill in 1988
8. The hamlet of Walton
9. Walton House, Walton Road
10. Walton Mill
11. Market Square in the 1860s
12. 1809 survey of the town centre
13. The *White Hart Inn*, in Market Square
14. Sale of building materials from the *White Hart Inn*, 1864
15. The Corn Exchange
16. Market Square, *c.*1870
17. The top of the Market Square, *c.*1870
18. Queen Victoria's visit, 1890
19. Ceremonial arch, Great Western Street
20. Arch at the top of Market Square
21. Arch at Kingsbury
22. Market Square in 1901
23. Looking towards the County Hall, 1901
24. The north end of the Market Square, *c.*1900
25. The statue of John Hampden
26. Unveiling the War Memorial, 1921
27. The top of the Market Square, 1921
28. The new Midland Bank
29. The *Bull's Head*, Market Square
30. Market day in the 1930s
31. The cattle market in 1944
32. The 'Pepper Pots'
33. An auction at the cattle market, 1987
34. The market in Friar's Square, 1989
35. The *Bull's Head*
36. The *King's Head*
37. The *King's Head*, 1921
38. The *Dark Lantern*
39. The *Bell*, 1921
40 & 41. The *Greyhound*
42. The *Angel*, Kingsbury
43. George White's cart from Long Crendon
44. The *Red Lion*, Kingsbury
45. An 1809 survey of Kingsbury
46. The Victoria Club, Kingsbury
47. Kingsbury and Buckingham Street, 1938
48. Buckingham Street in 1949
49. High Street in 1921
50. Cambridge Street
51. Bourbon Street
52. Temple Street
53. George Street
54. Strip map of coach roads, 1675
55. Buckingham Street
56. Walton Street
57. Walton turnpike house, 1831
58. Sale of materials of the turnpike house, 1878
59. Jeffery's map of 1770
60. 'New Road'
61. Tring Villas, High Street
62. The *Crown Hotel*, Market Square
63. Bicester Road
64. Hartwell Road
65. White Hill
66. Cambridge Street
67. Turnpike gates marked on an 1834 map
68. Grand Union Canal in 1921
69. Canal Wharf
70. L.N.W.R. station, *c.*1860
71. Ex-L.M.S. 2-4-2 tank engine at Aylesbury, 1949
72. Ex-G.W.R. 2-6-2 tank engine at Aylesbury, 1948
73. Ex-L.N.E.R. 4-6-0 locomotives at Aylesbury, 1948
74. Waddesdon to Aylesbury bus
75. Hills & Partridge's mill, Walton
76. Aylesbury Brewery Co., Walton Street
77. Dell's brewery, Bourbon Street
78-80. Hazell, Watson & Viney's printing works
81. Anglo-Swiss Condensed Milk Factory
82. Walton Engine Works in 1912

83. Bifurcated rivet works
84. An advertisement for bifurcated rivets
85. International Alloys, Bicester Road
86. Klockner-Moeller, Gatehouse Industrial Estate
87 & 88. St Mary's church before and after restoration
89 & 90. Interior views of St Mary's church
91. Holy Trinity church, Walton
92. St John's church, Cambridge Street
93. Congregational church, Hale Leys
94. Old Congregational church, Castle Street
95. Friends' Meeting House, Rickford's Hill
96. Baptist Meeting House, Cambridge Street
97. The Roman Catholic 'iron room', High Street
98. Wesleyan chapel, Friarage Path
99. Wesleyan chapel, Buckingham Street
100. Aylesbury Grammar School
101. St Mary's school, Oxford Road
102. British School, Pebble Lane
103. Queen's Park County School
104. Queen's Park School in the 1950s
105. The new Grammar School, Walton Road
106. The Grange School
107. The old workhouse next to the churchyard

108. Site of parish workhouse, Oxford Road
109. The Union Workhouse, Bierton Road
110. The County Gaol
111 & 112. The Infirmary
113. The County Hall
114. Walton Street before the building of the new County Offices
115. Laying the foundation stone of the new County Offices, 1928
116. New County Offices, Walton Street
117. The new County Hall under construction, 1964
118. Aylesbury U.D.C., 1908
119. The Public Baths
120. Vale Park
121. Vale Pool
122. The growth of Aylesbury since 1801
123. Victorian housing in the High Street
124. Queen's Park
125. Wendover Road
126. Victoria Park
127. Bierton Hill
128. Moore Avenue, Southcourt
129. Tring Road
130. Stonehaven Road
131. Westmorland Avenue

Acknowledgements

The majority of the photographs used in this book are from the extensive collection of the County Reference Library in Aylesbury. This collection was greatly enlarged in 1992 with the purchase of the Buckinghamshire originals of the former post card publishers, Francis Frith & Co. The glass negatives of these photographs are now preserved at Birmingham Reference Library. Thanks are due to Philip Allen, who was until recently in charge of Birmingham's special collections, for his advice at the time of purchase of these photographs and for permission to use those which are still in copyright.

Thanks are also due to the Buckinghamshire County Museum for permission to reproduce the photographs numbered 43 and 70 in the text, to Buckinghamshire County Record Office for illustrations 4, 57, 58 and 108, to the Bucks Herald for illustration 33 and to Aylesbury Vale District Council for illustration 123.

Mr. J. C. Venn of Great Missenden has kindly made available his own photographs and those of the late Stanley Freese. These are illustrations 7, 31, 34, 38, 40, 41, 47, 48, 53, 71-73, 76 and 130. Mr. Richard Johnson of Aylesbury has kindly contributed numbers 24, 25, 30, 35, 56, 61, 63, 64, 66, 75, 82, 83, 92, 97, 105, 110, 123-25, and 127-29. Mr. David Bailey provided illustration 51 and Dr. G. C. Farnell number 74.

Mr. Alan Dell, as always, gave useful information and encouragement.

The authors wish to thank their colleagues, both past and present, in both the County Record Office and County Reference Library, for their tolerance and support.

Introduction

Early History

The place-name Aylesbury, first recorded in the sixth century, derives from Aegel's burh, or fortress. Recent excavations have confirmed that the reference is to a pre-existing Celtic iron age hill fort, the hill in question being the rounded outcrop of soft Portland limestone on which the historic centre is situated. The hamlet of Walton in Aylesbury parish lies on a similar outcrop; it lies a little to the south of the town on the other side of the stream called the Bear Brook, one of several tributaries of the river Thame which meander through the clay Vale in the vicinity of Aylesbury.

Since Aylesbury lies on the Akeman Street, the present A41, it is not surprising that traces of Roman presence have been found, but there is very little evidence of actual Roman settlement in the town area and it seems certain that the Saxons when they arrived found the site unoccupied and under cultivation. Archaeological evidence of Saxon settlement is most abundant at Walton, where very early sunken circular huts, some possibly dating from the fifth century, have been unearthed. These particular Saxons were probably not invaders but mercenaries hired by the Romano-British authorities to guard the line of Akeman Street. Extensive Saxon settlement in the Aylesbury area generally is not found until the end of the sixth century. A puzzling entry in the Anglo-Saxon Chronicle under the year 571 records that Aylesbury was one of four towns captured from the Britons by the Anglo-Saxon leader, Cuthwulf, suggesting that the area immediately to the north west of the Chiltern hills had hitherto remained British, apart from earlier colonies of imported Saxon mercenaries.

By the mid-seventh century the Aylesbury area had been brought within the ambit of the expanded kingdom of Mercia and was a centre for the penetration of the Chiltern woodlands and pastures. The conversion of the Mercian kings to Christianity led to the founding of a network of 'minster', or missionary churches to evangelise their newly-acquired lands. The Aylesbury minster is thought to have been founded by King Wulfhere, 657-674, who installed his sister Edith as abbess. With Edith is associated her niece and pupil, Osyth, Aylesbury's patron saint. Osyth was born not at Aylesbury but at nearby Quarrendon, where her father Frithuwold, a sub-king of the Mercians, had his residence.

The minster was located within the compass of the ancient hill fort on or near the site of the present 13th-century parish church of St Mary. Confirmation of its status is provided by the discovery of a large number of mid-Saxon burials over a wide area to the south and south east of the present churchyard dating back at least to the eighth century.

Because it served a large tract of countryside Aylesbury's church was originally well endowed with lands and customary rights, references to which are found in Domesday Book. This privileged status was gradually eroded by the emergence of a network of local parish churches and by the intervention of the diocesan authorities. Most of the lands were eventually applied to endow the cathedral church of Lincoln and its prebendaries.

By the late 10th century Aylesbury had passed into the possession of the Anglo-Saxon kings and was to remain part of the royal demesne until 1204. It acquired a mint for coinage—one of only two in the county—and about the same period was enclosed within a defensive ditch, the southern boundary of which followed the line of Bourbon Street. To this period too must probably be dated the diversion of Akeman Street from its direct route, turning through Walton and entering the town from the south by Walton Street, the line it was to follow until the early 19th century.

In Domesday Book Aylesbury is listed first among the king's lands within the county. Walton is not separately mentioned and most of Bierton seems also to be included with Aylesbury. The entry lists toll valued at £10, 20 villeins, 24 borders or smallholders, two slaves and a freeholder holding one virgate of land 'who always serves the king's sheriff', together with two mills, arable land sufficient for 16 ploughs, with four more possible, and meadow enough for eight ploughs.

The inclusion of toll is rare evidence of the existence of an important market at this date. Mention of the sheriff suggests that Aylesbury already had a special place in the royal administration of the shire in 1086. Doubtless because of its central position, the Normans clearly preferred Aylesbury to Buckingham, the nominal county town, for this purpose for the county gaol—for which the sheriff was responsible—was located there from at least the 12th century.

There is some evidence that Aylesbury also had a castle during the Norman period. It was probably of short-lived motte and bailey construction, similar to those of which traces survive at nearby Whitchurch and Weston Turville, erected either in the immediate aftermath of the Conquest, or during the civil strife of the early 12th century. It was evidently located within the late Anglo-Saxon fortifications in the area later known as the Castle Fee, bounded by Bourbon Street, Temple Street, Temple Square and Rickford's Hill.

The Evolution of the Street Pattern

Aylesbury remained a royal manor for the whole of the 12th century. It was a formative period. New small-scale feudal landholdings were created, hospitals were founded and the physical limits of the town were extended and defined. In the process the basic pattern for urban development until the 19th century was established, though many of the details remain obscure.

The new landholdings took the form of miniature 'fees', or manors, created by royal grant or by subinfeudation in or around the reign of Henry II, who visited Aylesbury at least once. They included the Castle Fee already mentioned, which was held of the principal manor, and the better-documented Otterer's Fee, one of two 'petty serjeanties' held directly of the king by personal services. The Otterer's Fee was granted by Henry to his otter hunter, Roger Foll, around 1179 in return for providing the king with straw for his bed and floor covering for his residence three times yearly if required. 'Otterell's Lane' is mentioned in the 15th century. It lay in the vicinity of Green End, but its precise location cannot now be identified.

Otterer's Fee and Castle Fee are both referred to as distinct precincts in 13th-century deeds, together with Lord's Fee (the principal manor) and Church Fee. The latter almost certainly represents part of the original endowment of Aylesbury church. By the 13th century it constituted the prebend of Aylesbury in the cathedral church of Lincoln. Unlike the other minor fees, it survived into modern times by the names of Prebendal Manor, Rectory Manor and more colloquially, Parson's Fee—a name which now attaches to the lane in which The Prebendal, the former manor house, is situated. From early times the manor was leased out on long lease to a succession of lay tenants. Its 19th-century bounds show that it comprised some 8-10 acres embracing the church and its immediate vicinity, bounded on the south by Kingsbury and Castle Street.

Although, as has been seen, the origins of Aylesbury's market are lost in the mists of antiquity, the market place itself is first mentioned in the 13th century. It may well date back to the late 12th century, but there is no certainty about this. It was clearly a piece of deliberate planning consisting of a large rectangle of land situated on sloping ground immediately south east of the Anglo-Saxon town and extending on both sides of Walton Street, the principal thoroughfare. In the course of the later middle ages its size was gradually reduced by encroachment until by the late 16th century Silver Street and the complex of lanes and alleys around it was occupying much of its western half. This area changed little until its redevelopment in the 1960s.

Meanwhile the Anglo-Saxon cemetery was also being encroached upon from the south and east and specifically in the vicinity of the present George Street and the area between Castle Street and Church Street. The cemetery had probably once extended as far east as Kingsbury, 'the king's fortified manor house'. But by the early 14th century, when the name is first met with, Kingsbury appears to be an open area; the manor house and its appurtenances are later found occupying an adjacent site on the north west extending over several acres and taking in the area now occupied by Ripon Street and Granville Street. Later Kingsbury was itself encroached upon; the island of buildings which now separates it from Buckingham Street was already in existence by the end of the 16th century and probably much earlier.

Another open space which appears to have been encroached upon is Green End, now represented by a small length of roadway at Rickfords Hill, but probably of much greater extent in the 14th century, when the first references to it are found.

Aylesbury's latest medieval precinct to come into existence was the Friarage, consisting of the Franciscan friary, founded in the 1380s, and its landed endowment. The friary itself with its church, cloister and other buildings and its small cemetery adjoining was sited close to the market place on the present Rickford's Hill, alongside the still-existing Friars Path (now Friarage Passage). Its enclosed lands formed a long wedge bounded on the west by the Bear Brook and extending from Walton Street in the south almost as far as the Oxford Road. Among the amenities were fishponds, a bakehouse, a brewhouse and 'a little close called Paradise'. The Friarage retained much of its integrity until the advent of the railways in the 19th century.

Medieval, Religious and Charitable Organisations

The earliest distinctively urban institutions to emerge in Aylesbury, and the first to owe their existence to the inhabitants themselves, were the 12th-century hospitals of St Leonard and St John Baptist. They were said to have been founded by 'certain men of Aylesbury' with the confirmation of Henry I and Henry II; they were certainly in existence by the early 13th century. As was customary for a leper hospital, St Leonard's was situated outside the town on the Oxford Road side, where it gave its name to the Spittle mill, the Domesday mill on the Bear Brook. The hospital of St John Baptist was located in, or close to, the north-west side of the market place. Both hospitals had small endowments of land which—at least in the case of St Leonard's—were augmented by gifts to the 'leper brethren and sisters'.

Aylesbury's two hospitals may have been casualties of the Black Death or the other plagues which followed it, for in 1362 they were reported to be in an abandoned condition. Revival followed and in 1384 they were united in a single foundation which eventually, in the late 15th century, came under the control of the fraternity of the Virgin Mary.

Reference has already been made to the Franciscan friary, founded by 1386. It owed its existence to the 3rd earl of Ormond, who provided the site and an endowment of land; but the money required to build the church and cloister was the gift of a wealthy Winchester merchant following a petition by the friars to King Richard II. A few years later one of the Aylesbury friars was to suffer death for refusing to renounce his allegiance to the deposed Richard, boldly telling the usurping Henry IV to his face that he regarded him as merely the duke of Lancaster. On its dissolution in October 1538 the friary was reported to be poor and in debt with no goods of value, though the friary church was in good condition. There were nine friars living in it.

In contrast to the friary, the gild or fraternity of the Virgin Mary was a religious foundation which consisted solely of laymen and parishioners of Aylesbury coming together for spiritual and charitable purposes. Although formally licensed in 1450, it had apparently been in existence for some time before this date. Three of the seven founders named in the royal grant were members of the Baldwin family. The fraternity was given the right to maintain a chantry chaplain to celebrate mass in the parish church for the benefit of the souls of its members living and dead, to acquire property, to wear a distinctive dress at its meetings, to elect three wardens or masters annually and to have its own seal.

By the 1480s the fraternity had acquired a long list of properties, including the endowments of the two hospitals and a 'brotherhood house next the churchyard'. The latter building has recently been identified as forming part of the present county museum in Church Street. Timber dating techniques place its construction in the 1470s; amazingly, much of the original structure is still intact.

The fraternity evidently had a wide membership and its importance in the life of the town must have been very great. Its dissolution in 1547 and the loss of its considerable property represented little short of a catastrophe for the inhabitants.

The Lordship of Aylesbury

For most of the middle ages the manor of Aylesbury was a unit within a large territorial estate, first the estate of the Fitz Johns, descendants of Geoffrey Fitz Peter, earl of Essex, to whom King John had granted the manor in 1204, and later that of the Butlers, earls of Ormond, Anglo-Irish lords who inherited in 1332. Subjection to such mighty overlords may explain why the town failed to acquire borough status, the kind of limited control of its own affairs which Wycombe, for example, won for itself by the early 13th century.

The lord's principal local agent was the manorial bailiff, usually also one of the tenants, who was responsible for administering the demesne lands and buildings and gathering in the rents due from the manorial tenants. The Aylesbury bailiff about whom most is known is John Balky whose notebook gives a vivid insight into his daily activities during his period of office in the 1460s.

The lord's demesne, or home farm, comprised a large proportion of the total arable and meadow land within the manor. In the 14th century it was worked by a permanent staff of hired labourers under the direction of the bailiff, assisted by the customary labour services which the manorial tenants were bound to supply at peak times of the year. Surplus grain, hay and wool were sold for the lord's profit.

In the 1340s there were violent disputes with the tenants over pasture, but the situation seems to have eased with the general decline in population in the years following the appearance of the Black Death in 1349. Balky's notebook indicates that by the 1460s large-scale direct farming of the demesne had ceased and demesne pasture, meadow and arable were being rented out piecemeal to the tenants on an annual basis.

The arable lands of lord and tenants alike were distributed in strips within great open fields. The names, and possibly the number, of the open fields varied over the centuries. In the 17th century there were at least seven. Today Dunsham field is commemorated by Dunsham Lane and Aldenham field by Ardenham House at Bicester Road. Walton had its own separate set of open fields controlled by the prebendal manor of Walton.

The regulation of the open fields and of the good government of the town was effected through the manorial courts, of which there were several, the most important being the court leet, or view of frankpledge, which had jurisdiction over assaults and other minor breaches of the peace. In the course of the 15th century the court leet seems to have become more assertive in proclaiming its right to act on behalf of the whole community. In 1499, for example, it ordered that the court rolls and documents which were kept in the church were in future to be stored in a chest with two locks, one key to be held by the lord or his deputy and the other by the masters of the Fraternity of the Blessed Virgin.

In 1449 James Butler (1420-1461), 5th earl of Ormond, was granted an English peerage as earl of Wiltshire and in 1455 was made Lord High Treasurer of England. He thus became a protagonist in the Wars of the Roses on the side of the house of Lancaster and paid the penalty when he was beheaded after the battle of Towton in 1461. His estates were forfeited to the crown and were regranted to the Yorkist, Henry Bourchier (d.1483), created earl of Essex by Edward IV.

Following the accession of Henry VII in 1485 the earl of Wiltshire's former estates — Aylesbury among them—were restored to his younger brother, Thomas, 7th earl of Ormond. When Thomas died at an advanced age in 1515 without male heirs, Aylesbury, together with the other English lands, descended to his daughter Margaret, wife of Sir William Boleyn. Their son Thomas, created earl of Wiltshire and Ormond by Henry VIII in 1529, was the father of Queen Anne Boleyn.

The downfall of the Boleyns in 1536 provided an opportunity for Aylesbury's leading citizen, the lawyer Sir John Baldwin. He, who had been the late queen's judge, was able to purchase the manor from her father in 1538, thus becoming the first ever resident lord of the manor. The Baldwin connection with Aylesbury went back to the 14th century. They had helped to found the Fraternity in 1450 and were the lords of the minor manors of Castle Fee, Otterer's Fee and of Bawd's Fee in Walton.

In 1541 Baldwin obtained a grant of the former friary buildings and lands, together with other monastic property. The conventual buildings were converted for use as his residence. The former manor house in Kingsbury had long since become the *Bull Inn*; it later became a farmhouse.

On Baldwin's death in 1545 his lands descended to his two grandchildren, both minors, one of whom, Sir Thomas Pakington, of Hampton Lovett in Worcestershire, eventually obtained sole possession of Aylesbury in 1551. He was energetic in defending what he saw as his rights against the inhabitants of Aylesbury. When, in 1552, the tenants drew up a customal, declaring their traditional claims to have access to the lord's meadow and pasture at Haydon Hill at favourable fixed rates of payment, a bitter dispute ensued, for Pakington well knew that fixed rents were rapidly losing their value owing to inflation.

In 1554, while the conflict was still at its height, the townsmen obtained a charter of incorporation from Queen Mary, ostensibly as a reward for their loyalty in having promptly rallied to the Queen on her disputed succession to the throne.

The first town bailiff, or mayor, named in the charter was John Walwyn, a minor landowner who had taken a leading role in the dispute over pasture. Also named were nine other aldermen and twelve principal burgesses, making a common council of 22 to run the affairs of the newly created borough.

It looked as if the townsmen had at last succeeded in winning their independence, but alas, it was not to be. The opposition of the lord of the manor apparently proved too strong for the infant corporation. There is evidence that Walwyn had two successors, but after that nothing more is heard of the corporation nor the charter, and the manorial courts continued to function as before. As time went on their role in the government of the town was increasingly superseded by the justices of the peace and by the parish vestry. Nevertheless, the constables, who were the principal law enforcement officers of the town, continued to be appointed in the manor court until well into the 19th century.

The dispute over pasture rights was still rumbling on at the end of the century, but the lord had his way and Haydon Hill was eventually enclosed soon after 1600. By this time the remainder of the demesne was being leased in sizeable units at economic rents to a small group of tenant farmers and a new model of estate management was evolving.

During the Civil War Aylesbury was fortified and garrisoned by regular Parliamentary troops who remained in occupation until 1646. Since for much of this time the loyalist headquarters were at Oxford, the town was subject to constant skirmishing and the threat of attack.

The victory of Parliament in 1645 brought an opportunity to pay off old scores, for Sir John Pakington, 2nd baronet (1620-1680), the then lord of the manor, had sided with the King and in consequence had suffered the sequestration of his estates, redeemable eventually only on payment of a crippling fine. In 1649 eighty-eight inhabitants petitioned parliament for the return of their pasture called Haydon Hill which, it was alleged, had been given them by the crown and of which Sir Thomas Pakington 'by cunning devices' had deprived them, together with their charter of incorporation. Parliament complied and as a result Haydon Hill, together with the market, fairs and market tolls, was conveyed to trustees for the town.

At the Restoration Pakington succeeded in recovering Haydon Hill on the grounds that the conveyance had been made under duress. But his manor house, which had been pulled down to make fortifications, was never rebuilt and the Pakingtons were henceforth absentee landlords. As absentees their influence was chiefly manifested in connection with the election of Aylesbury's two MPs—for despite the loss of its corporation the town continued to be a parliamentary borough—by means of their control over the appointment of the constables, who were the official returning officers. The celebrated legal case of Ashby versus White, which sparked off a constitutional crisis in the opening years of the 18th century, arose out of the refusal of the Aylesbury constables to accept the vote of Matthew Ashby, an alehouse keeper. After 1715 the lord's influence was less dominant and elections were increasingly decided by wholesale bribery. Eventually, corruption in the election of 1802—known locally as 'Bent's election' from the name of one of the candidates—won Aylesbury the dubious distinction of its very own Reform Act, designed to discourage bribery by greatly enlarging the boundaries of the constituency.

In 1772 the parish of Aylesbury, except Walton, was enclosed by private Act of Parliament. A total of 1,740 acres was affected, including old inclosures. Two thirds of the total (1,226 acres) was allotted in compact blocks to seven landowners. The most striking development was the creation of a completely new landholding of 272 acres which was allotted to the prebendary of Aylesbury as rector in lieu of his rectorial tithes. This was the origin of the Prebendal farm on the west side of the town.

In Walton, where small holdings were proportionally more numerous than in Aylesbury proper, inclosure was delayed another 30 years until 1800. The largest single landowner was the prebendary of Heydour-cum-Walton, lord of the manor of Walton, who received 200 acres for Walton Court farm.

As happened in the Vale generally, the enclosures helped to accelerate the trend away from mixed arable farming to a less labour-intensive pastoral economy, to which the heavy soils were well suited.

In 1801 Sir John Pakington, baronet, sold the manor and the estate, then comprising some 700 acres, to George, marquess of Buckingham, the head of the powerful Grenville family of Stowe near Buckingham, who was anxious to increase his political influence in the town. The Grenvilles, who were compelled by bankruptcy to sell their Aylesbury property in 1848, were the last lords of the manor who were also major landowners.

The Urban Economy and Society

For the greater part of its history Aylesbury was quintessentially a market town, engaged in providing the inhabitants of the Vale with the kinds of goods and services that the term implies at different periods. Personal names of the 13th and 14th centuries show a fairly wide range of specialised crafts and occupations including draper, tailor, salter, smith, poulterer, cooper, spicer, goldsmith, vintner, carpenter, carter and shepherd. By the 14th and 15th centuries references are found to particular locations within the town which are associated with certain specific trades. These are Cordwainers (i.e. leatherworkers) Row, Drapers Row, Butchers Row otherwise the Shambles, and Bakers Row, all situated in the immediate vicinity of the market place. All four trades were significant in the town's economy in following centuries. As late as 1851, for example, no fewer than 22 slaughterhouses were registered and there were still half that number in 1930.

Information about the market itself is scanty and indirect, but from early times grain, livestock and local produce probably accounted for the major share of the business done. Mention of the rother (ie cattle) fair and the horse fair, both located within the market place, shows the importance of livestock. Wool was sold in the 13th century, but is not mentioned thereafter until the 19th century. Goods were displayed for sale on stalls which paid a rent to the lord of the manor and may have been provided by him. In the 15th century the shoemakers paid a rent to ensure that 'no foreign shoemakers should sell their shoes on the north side of the King's gaol during times of fairs and markets'.

The importance of victualling generally is seen in the numbers of retailers routinely fined at manor courts in 1454-55. Up to 10 butchers, six bakers, 15 fishmongers, 29 alesellers, 16 brewers and four innkeepers were fined at a single session, though the same names often recur in more than one category. Apart from the *Bull* in Kingsbury the principal inns and taverns were situated in the market place. *The George, King's Head, Crown* and *Bell* are all mentioned in the 15th century and the *White Hart* in the 16th. In a return of 1577 Aylesbury is credited with· four inns, 25 alehouses and two victuallers. In 1753 there were 29 licensed victuallers. In the 1870s there were 60 public houses and 27 beerhouses.

In 1327 taxation records show that Aylesbury ranked first among the Buckinghamshire towns—none of them of any great size or importance on a national scale—in terms of aggregate wealth. In 1343 the annual value of the market to the lord was estimated at £24, a considerable sum. By the 15th century the rent had fallen to £10, suggesting an overall contraction in trade. Nevertheless, on the evidence of the subsidy roll of 1524-5, together with that of the 1522 muster roll, Aylesbury was then a relatively prosperous place, ranking just second to Wycombe in the league table of the county's towns in terms of total wealth and with an estimated total population of between 800 and 1,000. Wealth was fairly evenly distributed: 26 per cent of taxpayers were assessed on goods or wages worth £1: a further 40 per cent at £1-£2; while of the remaining 33 per cent only five per cent were taxed at £20 or above.

The second and third quarters of the 16th century were marked by epidemic disease and communal strife, but the grant of an additional Monday market and two additional annual fairs to the lord of the manor in 1579 suggests a growth of trade over the period as a whole, though the extra market seems to have been short-lived. The antiquary, William Leland (1551-1623) who visited the town before 1586, described it as 'a very fair Market-town, large and pretty populous, surrounded with a great number of pleasant meadows and pastures ...' He noted that 'The greatest repute it now hath is for Cattel' and remarked on the vast numbers of sheep grazed at Quarrendon and elsewhere in the vicinity. Conversion of tillage in favour of large-scale sheep pasturing, often accompanied by depopulation, had occurred in a number of Vale parishes over the preceding century.

During the first half of the 17th century the population of the town remained fairly stationary and outbreaks of plague were frequent, but from 1659 there is a gradual rise of the annual rate of baptisms. Metal tokens issued by local tradesmen between 1656 and 1670 to overcome a shortage of small change give an insight into commercial activity at this time. Of a total of 16 'tokeners', five were described as mercers or drapers, four as grocers and/or tallow chandlers, three as innkeepers, and there were also a brewer, a stationer and a coffee house keeper, the latter a reminder of the recent growth in overseas trade.

By the end of the century the population appears to have been increasing quite rapidly. This was partly at least as a result of immigration into the town, for there is mention of cottage building on waste ground on the fringes of the town at Oxford Road and the present Cambridge Street. Many of the newcomers were very poor. It was the need to provide employment for this large group of indigent people which provided the spur to the emergence of the cottage industries of lacemaking and duck breeding in this period. Both were directed to the London market and both became closely associated with Aylesbury during the 18th century.

Bone lacemaking, a 'putting out' industry, is first mentioned in the accounts of the overseers of the poor for the parish in 1672; it evidently developed rapidly, for in 1698 it was claimed that there were 429 persons in Aylesbury 'which get their living by making of lace'. Those employed were women and young children. Evidence for duck breeding is later, but the trade seems to have started before 1700 for the name 'Duck End', used to describe the low-lying area of the old Oxford Road near the bottom of Castle Street, is found in the 1690s. Lacemaking continued to be important in the local economy until the invention of machine made lace in the early 19th century. Duck-breeding, in contrast, was given a new lease of life by the railways, though by this time most of the ducks were reared in surrounding villages.

A further impetus was given to trade by the general increase in road traffic after 1660, evidenced by the establishment of a regular coach service to London and the appointment of a postmaster. The increasing tendency to concentrate the twice-yearly assize courts and the quarterly meetings of the magistrates of the county in general session in Aylesbury also brought money into the town. These gatherings were big social occasions accompanied by a good deal of wining and dining and other forms of entertainment. The demand for better roads led to the setting up of the Wendover to Buckingham turnpike trust in 1721, the first of many such trusts established in this period.

Descriptions of Aylesbury during the 18th century give an impression of prosperity. Cox's *Magna Brittania*, 1720, praises its market which, he says, 'abounds will all sorts of provisions, much better and cheaper than any other so near London ... which is owing to the rich Vale adjoining'. Defoe confirmed its pre-eminence as the principal market town in the county and noted its 'very noble' market in corn. Doctor Pococke, who passed through in 1750, summed up the town's economy succinctly: 'The chief support of the town is the market, thoroughfare and assizes'. He also remarked on the duck industry: 'The poor people of this town are supported by breeding young ducks; four carts go with them every Saturday to London ... they hatch 'em under hens'. The *Universal British Directory*, 1792, which lists an astonishing variety of trades and crafts, mentions no fewer than six annual fairs and gives details of stage coaches and carriers connecting to London, Birmingham, Bicester, Brackley and elsewhere.

Aylesbury's 18th-century prosperity is reflected in its surviving buildings. Many of the houses in Church Street, Temple Square and vicinity, where the town's elite of lawyers, medical men and the more prosperous tradesmen tended to congregate, were rebuilt—or more often refronted—in dignified brick from the 1720s onward. Examples are No. 10 Temple Square, erected by Jacob Dell the elder and his nephew of the same name, both maltsters, and Ceely House in Church Street, the former Brotherhood house of the medieval Fraternity and now part of the County Museum, which was refronted by Hugh Barker Bell, a lawyer, in the mid-18th century and converted into an elegant town house.

More imposing residences were the Prebendal House, built around 1710 by William Mead, a wealthy retired London merchant, and enlarged and beautified by John Wilkes (1727-1797), the politician and rake, who was MP for Aylesbury from 1757 to 1764. Ardenham House, built for the blue-stocking Miss Welsh to the design of her brother-in-law, the sculptor Joseph Nollekens (1737-1823); and Green End House, with its classical facade of stuccoed brick, the home of William Rickford (1768-1854), joint founder with his father, a grocer, of Aylesbury's first bank.

Notable public buildings of the period are the Free Grammar School, re-endowed by Henry Phillips of London and completed in 1719, and the County Hall, begun in 1722 but not finally completed until 1740. As originally designed, the County Hall incorporated assize courts and a new county gaol (pulled down in 1847). It effectively set the seal on Aylesbury's claim to be the county town, though Buckingham continued its resistance and even succeeded in having an Act of Parliament passed in 1748 requiring the summer assize to be held there.

The 19th century and After

By the year 1800 the population of Aylesbury had topped the 3,000 mark and was increasing steadily; it would double in size by mid-century. Increased numbers brought increased problems. Already by the 1780s and 1790s chronic unemployment was placing a heavy burden on the poor rate and its effects were to be exacerbated by the decline of the lace industry in the 1820s. In the past Aylesbury's prosperity had owed much to its network of road links, both local and long-distance. In the 19th century its development, geographical as well as economic, was to be closely bound up with rapid changes in the pattern and mode of communications which affected the country generally, bringing new opportunities and new challenges.

The first of these changes was the arrival of the canal. The completion in 1805 of the Grand Junction Canal from the Oxford Canal at Braunston in Northamptonshire to the Thames at Brentford provided a final link in a nationwide system of inland waterways uniting London to the Trent, Severn and Mersey. Its potential importance for trade was not lost on the leading citizens of Aylesbury, who as early as 1792 were petitioning for the construction of a collateral cut. The Aylesbury 'arm' from the Grand Junction at Marsworth was not in fact completed until 1814. Its terminus was at Walton Street, conveniently close to the market place.

Meanwhile the turnpiking of local roads and cross routes was continuing. In 1826 the Sparrows Herne turnpike trust was responsible for diverting the A41 on the east side of the town into its original, Roman, track, thus creating the present High Street (then called New Road), stretching from Walton Road to the market place and providing a more direct access to the town from the south east. Improvements in the techniques of road-making brought yet more and faster traffic. By the mid-1820s Aylesbury had 12 coaches passing through every 24 hours and it was possible to go to London and back in a single day.

But the days of coaching were almost over. In 1833 the London and Birmingham Railway Act was passed and the railway line—the first of the trunk routes—was opened in 1838. As had happened earlier with the canal, opposition from landowners in the Chilterns led to the selection of a route which bypassed Aylesbury on the east. Once again the leading inhabitants rose to the situation and obtained their own Act for an Aylesbury branch railway which opened in June 1839. Its station was situated close to the new High Street.

By dramatically reducing the cost of coal and of other heavy goods, the canal and after it the railway had a big impact on living standards as well as on commerce. Looking back 50 years from 1842 John Gibbs, a liberal and a believer in 'progress', could point to great improvements in the amenities of the town since the 1790s. They included stone pavements in place of filthy, uneven road surfaces; gas lighting (introduced in 1834); local newspapers and banks (of which there were four in 1842); new public buildings and new shop-fronts in the market place. Among the new public buildings were a new market house, a county infirmary (later the Royal Buckinghamshire Hospital), opened in 1833 following an outbreak of cholera, and several nonconformist chapels. They would shortly be joined by a new union workhouse, a county gaol on the Bierton Road and a new parish church at Walton.

Gibbs also saw great improvements in religion, public morality and education in the same period, led in large part by a revival in nonconformity which had reached a low ebb in the latter part of the 18th century. One beneficial result had been that brutal sports and pastimes, such as bull-baiting, badger-baiting and cock-fighting, once popular with all classes, faded away in the face of opposition from the respectable.

The other side of the picture emerges in the report into sanitary conditions in Aylesbury published in 1849 by the General Board of Health following a public enquiry held under the Public Health Act of 1848. It reveals that the death rate was 24 per thousand and that the expectation of life at birth in the Aylesbury registration district was 28 years and three months, which, it is noted, was 4½ years less than in the Wycombe district. Prominent among the causes of death were preventible diseases such as diarrhoea, fever and dysentery. The principal contributory factors indicated were severe overcrowding, poor housing, inadequate sanitation and a deficiency of good water.

The immediate outcome of the 1849 report was the setting up of an elected Local Board of Health which became the principal governing body of the town until 1894, when it was succeeded by the Urban District Council, which in turn became the Aylesbury Borough Council in 1917. The Board was responsible for providing an acceptable sewage system which, however, was not completed until around 1870. It also promoted the provision of a piped water supply inaugurated in 1867, drawing water from the hills above Aston Clinton to the east of the town. The route taken by the water mains along the Tring Road was an important factor influencing building development at this period for it was to be many years before both services were available in all parts of the town.

Although its population had doubled since the beginning of the century, Aylesbury in 1849 was still virtually confined to its 1800 limits. Neither the canal nor the railway had generated any considerable development and even the new High Street remained empty of buildings for most of its length. This situation began to change in the second half of the century with the coming of industry on a large scale.

In 1870 the Aylesbury Condensed Milk Company, a new company with a new product, opened a factory on the Tring Road adjacent to the canal and with its own wharf. By the 1880s, as the Anglo-Swiss Condensed Milk Company (now Nestlés), it was employing 150 workers, many of them women, and consuming 104,000 gallons of local milk monthly. In contrast Hazell's printing works (later Hazell, Watson and Viney) began as a branch of a London-based firm in 1867, moving to a new purpose-built factory on the Tring Road in 1879. By the 1880s there were around 400 employees many of whom had migrated from London. Hazell's and Nestlés, together with the later arrivals Hunt Barnard (1898), another printing company, and the Bifurcated and Tubular Rivet Company (1910) were for many years the principal employers of labour in the town.

Agricultural prosperity in the 1850s and 1860s led to an expansion of the market and of trade generally. In 1863 a consortium of local people purchased the market rights from the then lord of the manor and formed the Aylesbury Market Company with an authorised capital of £18,000. This resulted in the erection of a spacious corn exchange or market buildings directly adjoining the County Hall on the site of the ancient *White Hart* inn. An open space for a new cattle market was provided at the rear together with a new approach road, Exchange Street, linking Walton Street and High Street, designed to ensure that cattle need no longer be driven through the centre of the town.

The onset of agricultural depression in the late 1870s led to a steep decline in the corn trade, but the cattle trade was less affected. In 1896 weekly sales of livestock averaged 470 sheep, 105 cattle and 125 pigs. In 1901 The Corn Exchange was purchased by the Urban District Council, along with the market rights, and was utilised in part as a town hall.

The physical expansion of the town after 1850 was at first gradual and mainly piecemeal in character, spreading along the existing roads and accompanied by some infilling of open spaces in the centre. Extensions of terrace housing took place along and adjacent to Cambridge Street and Bierton Road. Building development in High Street was also mainly residential in character, though of higher quality. By the end of the century, when the population had reached 9,243, medium-sized residential estates had begun to appear to the north and east in Bicester Road and Bierton Road and in Tring Road, close to the new factories.

Development on the south and west sides of the town was sparser and was largely determined by the railway. The Great Western Railway reached Aylesbury via High Wycombe and Princes Risborough in 1863. The new Town Station was built in the Friarage and a new street, Great Western Street, connected it to the Market Square. The station, rebuilt in 1925-26, was shared by the Aylesbury and Buckingham Railway, a local line opened in 1868, and by the Metropolitan Railway when it was finally extended to Aylesbury in 1892 to provide the first direct rail link to the capital. Aylesbury's rail network was completed in 1899 when the new Great Central Railway provided a main line route north to Manchester.

The physical expansion of the town was accompanied by an increase in the number of shops and small businesses, many of them supplying new or more specialised services, photography among them. It was a golden age for the small shopkeeper, as yet little affected by the multiple stores which were just beginning to appear. As in the past, food and clothing shops were particularly numerous. An increasing proportion of them were located in the upper High Street area, which was beginning to rival the Market Square as a shopping centre.

The rate of population growth was relatively slow during most of the inter-war period. Development now was characterised by the spread of large-scale, low-density municipal housing on the south-west and by ribbon development to the south and east which owed much to the increasing popularity of the motor car. Southcourt, begun in 1920 on land purchased from the Ecclesiastical Commissioners, was associated directly with slum clearance in White Hill and in other parts of the old town, carried out under national housing legislation.

There was a continued slow but steady growth in commerce and industry. The local authority had itself pioneered the use of electricity by setting up its own generating works in 1915. Originally designed for the purpose of street lighting, it made available a cheap source of power for industry. At the same time Aylesbury was benefiting from a big expansion in county administration and in local hospital services.

Characteristic of local business enterprise at this time is the firm of Webster and Cannon, builders, of Cambridge Street. First established in the 1880s, it had a work force of 500 in the 1930s and was responsible for many important commercial and public buildings in the town including the Rivet Works factory (1910), the Midland Bank in Market Square (1921), the County Council offices in Walton Street (1929) and the headquarters of the Buckinghamshire Constabulary in Exchange Street (1935). The firm, whose activities extended far beyond Aylesbury, had its own brickyard, as well as a mason's yard, joinery works and blacksmith's shop. It was wound up in 1987.

The Second World War was responsible for Aylesbury's most famous institution, Stoke Mandeville Hospital, built originally under wartime Emergency Medical Services arrangements. The National Spinal Injuries Centre, established there under the direction of Dr. Ludwig Guttman in 1944, has attained worldwide renown, as have the annual Stoke Mandeville paraplegic games which were first held in 1954. The war period also saw the start of an influx of new industries. The earliest was International Alloys, which gave Aylesbury its first and only experience of heavy industry. More typical was Air Trainers Ltd. (later Redifon Ltd), which began production in 1947 in the specialised field of flight simulation and had well over 500 employees by 1954. Many of these early arrivals were to cease trading or move away in the course of the 1970s and 1980s.

Council house building resumed during the post-war period. Southcourt again doubled in size during the 1950s, helped by the use of prefabricated housing. At the same time economic development was being promoted by the establishment of specialised industrial estates. Some 36 per cent of the labour force was now employed in industry, 25 per cent in commerce, finance and personal services and another 25 per cent in administration. In 1958 planned expansion began under an agreement for rehousing overspill population from the capital.

Up to now the fabric and much of the atmosphere of the historic market town had remained relatively intact. All this was to change in the early 1960s when a wholesale redevelopment of the Silver Street/Great Western Street area adjoining the Market Square was decided upon, inspired by the prevailing fashion and the 1952 Town Development Act. Friars Square, the new two-level town centre, was a fairly typical example of its kind and is itself currently. undergoing comprehensive redevelopment. The adjacent new County Council offices in Walton Street was designed as part of the same complex. A 12-storey tower block in uncompromising grey concrete, visible for miles across the Vale, its scale dwarfed all existing buildings including the parish church.

The 30 years between 1960 and 1990, during which the population of Aylesbury more than doubled to reach 50,000, were a period of unprecedented expansion. New housing estates crept out to and beyond the town boundaries on all sides. Massive office development in Walton Street and elsewhere proclaimed the arrival of major commercial enterprises, mostly in the field of insurance. Meanwhile the retail trade was completely transformed by the advent of supermarkets, and latterly superstores. The closure in 1987 of the cattle market severed the last significant link with the old market town days; it attracted relatively little attention at the time.

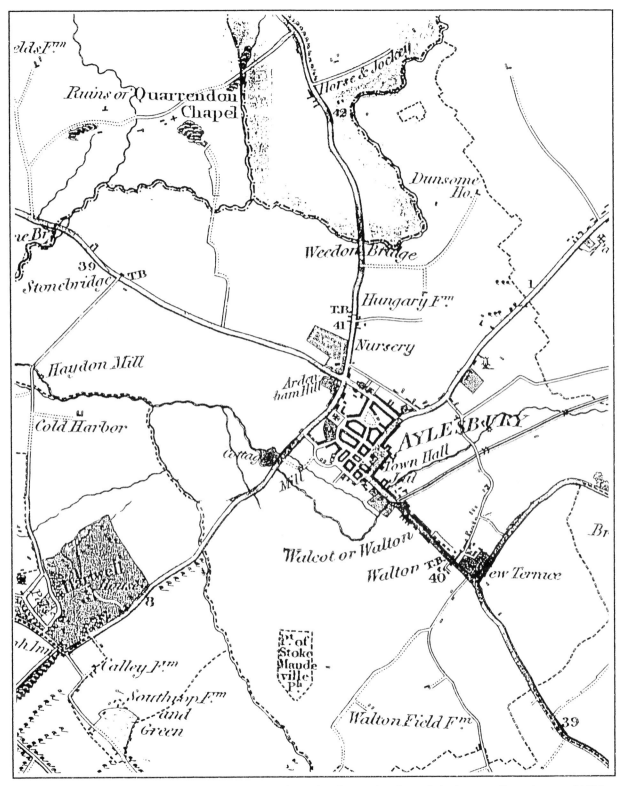

1. The extent of Aylesbury and its position at the crossing point of several main roads is shown on Bryant's map of 1824. The boundary, marked as a dotted line, follows streams on the west and north but to the south and east it zig-zags round the ends of the furlongs in the open fields of Stoke Mandeville, Weston Turville and Bierton.

Kingsbury Square, Aylesbury. W8482.

2. Many of Aylesbury's farmers would have been required to attend a manor court where changes in land holding, either by inheritance or sale, would be recorded. At the time of Domesday Book, the lord of the manor was the king and his manor house would have been in Kingsbury (meaning a fortified place belonging to the king). The probable site is that of the large five-bay building in this early photograph.

The Particulars and Conditions of Sale

OF THE VERY VALUABLE

FREEHOLD MANOR

OF

Aylesbury with Bierton,

WITH QUIT RENTS AMOUNTING TO £33. 9s. 2d. PER ANNUM, FINES, &c.

The MANOR of the RECTORY of AYLESBURY,

With the RIGHT OF APPOINTING CONSTABLES; also,

THE MANOR OF BROUGHTON STAVELY,

With QUIT RENTS amounting to £8. 5s. 7d. per Annum, FINES, &c.

THE TOLLS OF THE AYLESBURY MARKET, &c.

Let at EIGHTY-FIVE POUNDS per Annum.

The MANOR HOUSE, Garden & Land,

Extending from KINGSBURY to the High Road to BUCKINGHAM,

AND

FOUR DWELLING HOUSES ADJOINING.

THE BULL CLOSE,

A Valuable Piece of PASTURE LAND, eligible for BUILDING UPON,

AND ABUTTING ON THE TURNPIKE ROAD,

With Extensive Yard and Farming Buildings, in White Hill Street,

And *FIVE COTTAGES NEAR THE CHURCHYARD.*

ALSO

THE REVERSION after the death of Mr. BARTON, aged 64 Years,

TO A

Freehold House & Butcher's Shop, Slaughter House, &c.

IN THE BUCKINGHAM ROAD.

Which will be Sold by Auction,

BY MESSRS.

FAREBROTHER, CLARK and LYE

AT THE GEORGE INN, AYLESBURY,

On FRIDAY, the 5th day of MAY, 1848,

AT TEN FOR ELEVEN O'CLOCK PRECISELY.—IN LOTS.

Particulars may be had of Messrs. TINDAL and SON, Solicitors, Aylesbury; at the Place of Sale; Red Lion, Wendover;
Cobham Arms, Buckingham; Angel, Oxford; Bell, Winslow; of Messrs. LIGHTFOOT, ROBSON and LIGHTFOOT,
Solicitors, Castle Street, Leicester Square; at Garraways; and at Messrs. FAREBROTHER, CLARK and LYE's
Offices, 6, Lancaster Place, Strand.

3. Successive lords of the manor were absentees and their manor house became reduced in status. For a long period it was an inn named the *Bull* and the land to the rear was known until modern times as the Bull Close. This sale catalogue of 1848, when the lord of the manor was the bankrupt Duke of Buckingham, revives the term 'Manor House'.

4. The purchaser in 1848 was Acton Tindall, a local solicitor and Clerk of the Peace of the County of Buckingham. To underline his new position as lord of the manor he built a new house on Bierton Hill in 1851 and called it 'Manor House'. In 1927 the house was bought by the county council and turned into a hospital for mentally handicapped children. It was demolished in 1973.

5. The centre of the church estate in Aylesbury was the Prebendal House. The prebendary was an ecclesiastical official at the cathedral in Lincoln to whom the income of the Aylesbury estate was paid. He appointed a vicar to officiate at Aylesbury and rented out the Prebendal House. One of the tenants in the 18th century was the famous politician John Wilkes. The Prebendal House was sold in 1801 to redeem the land tax on the remaining church land and has been a gentleman's house and even a school.

6. The former vicarage, now called St Osyth's, adjoins the Prebendal House on Parson's Fee. The prebendary, or Parson as he was sometimes known, had the right to collect a tenth, or 'tithe' of the crops of other farmers in the parish. At the inclosure of Aylesbury in 1772 the prebendary received a 272-acre allotment of land either side of the Oxford Road in lieu of his right to collect tithes. The vicarage house appears to have been used as the farmhouse for this land until a new Prebendal Farm was built beside the Oxford Road in the mid-19th century. There is still a tithe barn behind St Osyth's.

7. Aylesbury had two mills in 1086. One of them was probably on the site of Spittle Mill seen here in 1988. Construction of the Grand Junction Canal, 1811-14, so affected the mill stream that the canal company bought the mill. The initials G.J.C.C. can still be seen on a datestone.

8. The hamlet of Walton was a distinct settlement from Aylesbury, separated in part by a stream locally known as the Bear Brook, and having its own common fields. This farmhouse, overlooking the pond, had a considerable number of strips in the open fields. At inclosure in 1800, the inclosure commissioners awarded the owners a single block of land of similar value.

9. This farmhouse was purchased in 1759 for use as a branch of the London Foundling Hospital. Children from far and wide were cared for here but the scheme failed when one of the members of the local committee, John Wilkes, was accused of embezzling the funds. It was rebuilt in the 19th century as Walton House by the wealthy Aylesbury solicitor Thomas Parrott. It was demolished around 1945 to make way for the Technical School.

10. Walton hamlet had its own corn mill powered by the Bear Brook and probably on the same site as the second mill mentioned at Domesday. It too was affected by the building of the canal and was purchased by the canal company.

11. Aylesbury Market Square was probably a product of medieval town planning, providing extra space for selling cattle and provisions. This 1860s view shows the Market House and shops which by then had encroached on the centre of the Square.

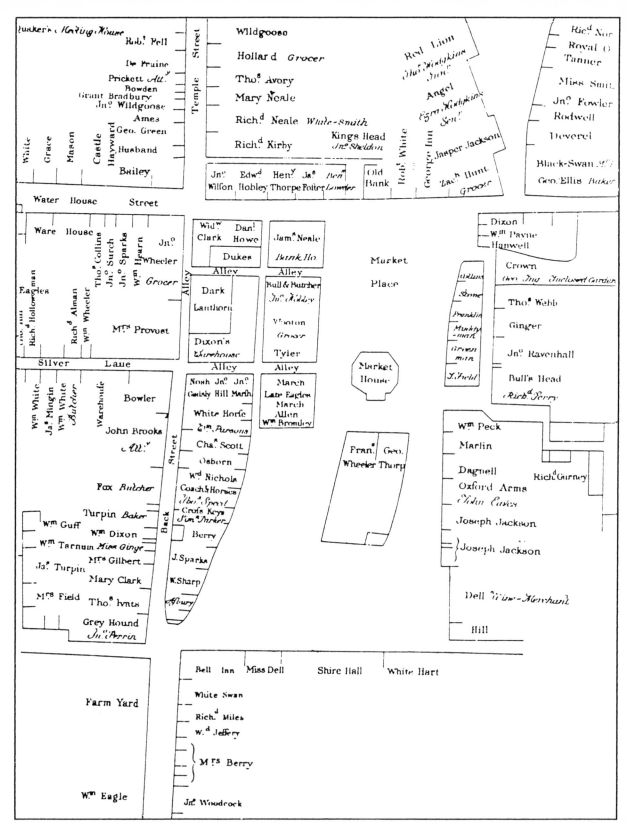

12. This 1809 survey of the town centre gives the names of all the tradesmen and shows the network of alleys between the various buildings which by then cluttered the Market Square.

13. The *White Hart Inn*, the principal coaching inn in Aylesbury, stood at the south-east corner of the Market Square. Its façade of Bath stone was said to have come from the demolished Eythrope House, Waddesdon, in 1814. The *White Hart* was itself demolished in 1864 to make way for the new Corn Exchange.

WHITE HART HOTEL,
AYLESBURY.

CATALOGUE

OF A PORTION OF THE SOUND

BUILDING
MATERIALS
AND EFFECTS,

OF THE

WHITE HART HOTEL, AYLESBURY,

TO BE SOLD BY AUCTION, BY

MR. ROBERT GIBBS,

ON THE PREMISES,

On **WEDNESDAY**, the 27th Day of **APRIL, 1864,**

AT ONE O'CLOCK IN THE AFTERNOON.

May be viewed at any time before the Sale, and Catalogues, with Conditions, had at the Office of the Auctioneer, Bourbon-Street, Aylesbury.

N.B.—The Turf on the Lawn and Gardens is now to be Sold at 2d. per Square Yard. Apply to Mr. French, on the Premises.

ROBERT GIBBS, PRINTER, BOURBON-STREET, AYLESBURY.

14. An advertisement for the sale of building materials of the *White Hart Inn*, 1864. The late proprietor, J. K. Fowler, was the author of three popular books on Aylesbury Vale events and characters.

15. The new Corn Exchange, built by the Aylesbury Market Company in 1865. The high hopes of the proprietors were never realised and the building was sold to the Aylesbury Urban District Council in 1901 as a town hall.

16. Aylesbury Market Square about 1870. The old Market House and the shops and houses in the centre have been demolished leaving the Square as empty as it must have been in medieval times.

17. A view from the top of the Market Square about 1870. The Square was once even larger, for the shops on the right are encroachments, masking earlier buildings which must have originally fronted the Square.

18. Aylesbury in party mood, decorated for the visit of Queen Victoria in 1890. Although she was en route for Baron Rothschild's Waddesdon Manor, her coach toured the centre of the town before leaving via the Bicester Road.

19. On leaving the railway station, the Queen's coach entered the Market Square via Great Western Street where the first of three ceremonial arches was erected.

20. The triumphal arch erected for the 1890 royal visit at the top of the Market Square. To the left is the Bucks & Oxon Union Bank.

21. Another commemorative arch to celebrate the 1890 royal visit, this one at the exit of Kingsbury.

22. Aylesbury Market Square in 1901. *Kelly's Directory* described the market as 'large and commodious' and 'abundantly supplied with meat, grain, cattle, pigs, poultry and other agricultural produce'.

23. Looking from the top of the Square towards the County Hall in 1901.

24. The north end of the Market Square around 1900. The scene is dominated by the *George Inn*, a serious rival to the *White Hart* for the coaching and commercial trade. It was demolished in 1935 to make way for a branch of Burtons.

25. This statue of John Hampden was erected in front of the *George Inn* in the Market Square in 1912. Hampden had played a key role in Parliamentary opposition to Charles I and was sent for trial for his refusal to pay 'ship money', one of the King's extraordinary taxes raised without Parliamentary approval. Hampden was killed early in the Civil War at Chalgrove Field, near Thame, in 1643.

26. Another prominent monument at the north of the Market Square is the First World War memorial, erected in 1921. The photograph shows the unveiling ceremony.

27. Looking from the top of the Market Square in 1921. Despite the opening of the cattle market through the Corn Exchange arches, cattle were still being sold in the Market Square until 1927.

28. Another view of the top of the Market Square showing the new Midland Bank, built in 1921.

29. Sheep being sold in the Market Square prior to 1927. The *Bull's Head Inn*, a favourite haunt of the carriers, can be seen in the background.

MARKET PLACE, AYLESBURY.(14)

30. Market day in the 1930s. The open market continued to be held in the Market Square until it was moved to the centre of the new Friar's Square shopping centre in 1967.

31. The cattle market was extended in 1927. It is seen here in 1944, viewed from the old County Offices in Walton Street.

32. The eight-sided auction rings were locally known as the pepper pots. The market closed in 1987 and the buildings were demolished the following year, but their style is reflected in the design of the Civic Centre.

33. One of the last auctions at the cattle market in 1987.

34. The open market in Friar's Square in 1989. Building work to put a spectacular glazed roof over the Square and to update its shops started in 1990 when the market stalls moved back to a repaved Market Square.

35. The antiquity of some of Aylesbury's pubs is suggested by their position on the perimeter of the medieval market place. The *Bull's Head* had been hidden behind stalls which became permanent buildings on the east of the Square, probably since medieval times. It was demolished in 1970 to be replaced by the Hale Leys shopping centre.

36. The façade of the *King's Head* marks the original building line to the north of the Market Square. It was probably an important private house before becoming an inn. The glass in the hall window contains the arms of King Henry VI and his Queen, Margaret of Anjou. William Wandesford, the owner in 1455, had served in the Queen's household and forfeited his estates in the Wars of the Roses.

37. The impressive ten-light oak mullioned window and the rather low coach or cart entrance feature in this 1921 view of the *King's Head*. The property was given to the National Trust in 1926 by the Rothschilds.

38. The site of the *Dark Lantern* must have been an encroachment on the west of the Market Square.

39. Aylesbury has lost most of the inns which used to serve the farmers and traders on market days, but the *Bell* survives at the corner of Walton Street. The photograph dates from 1921.

40. The *Greyhound Inn* occupied the corner of Silver Street and Great Western Street, both of which were destroyed in the 1960s redevelopment.

41. The *Greyhound* stood out from the building line of Great Western Street, making the entrance into the Market Square rather narrow.

42. Domesday Book assessors noted the value of Aylesbury's market tolls. The market was probably held in the churchyard or here in Kingsbury at that time. The *Angel Inn*, on the left of this turn-of-the-century picture, was the base for many of the carriers who brought goods and people to the market from villages as far as 25 miles away.

43. George White from Long Crendon came to the market on Wednesday and Saturday. His cart would be stationed at the *Angel Inn* where parcels for Long Crendon and Thame would be received.

44. The early 19th-century façade of the *Red Lion Inn*, Kingsbury, conceals an older building. The central gateway would have been used for coaches or, latterly, carriers' carts which stopped here on their way to London.

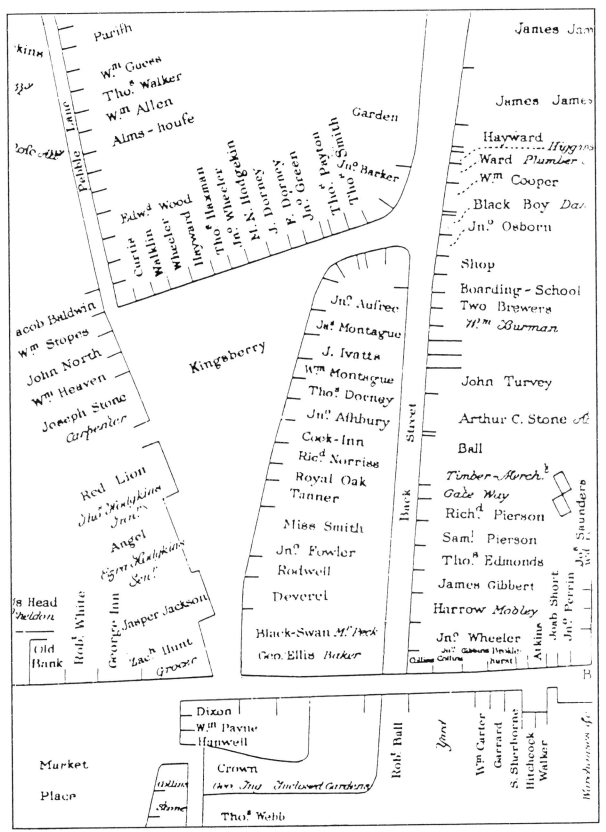

45. This 1809 survey of Kingsbury shows how much of the square was taken up by encroachments which became permanent buildings.

46. This out-of-scale addition to Kingsbury is the Victoria Club, built with Rothschild money at the time of Queen Victoria's Golden Jubilee.

47. The exit from Kingsbury into Buckingham Street was very narrow until the shops on the corner were demolished. This photograph was taken in 1938.

48. This 1949 view shows the backs of the shops on the east of the square fronting Buckingham Street, earlier known appropriately as Back Street. The Kingsbury Court shopping development now occupies part of this site.

49. Several Aylesbury streets have changed their names. The High Street, seen here in 1921, began life in 1826 as New Road, a diversion of the turnpike road to bring traffic from the Tring direction directly into the Market Square instead of coming in via Walton Street.

50. Cambridge Street, the main entrance to the town from the north-east, was formerly called Baker's, or more properly, Balky's Lane. The Balky family lived here in the 15th century and a John Balky was Bailiff of the Manor in the 1460s.

51. Bourbon Street was at one time named Waterhouse Lane after the building at its west end to which water was pumped up from the Mill Stream to be distributed in wooden pipes to houses in that part of the town. It was renamed Bourbon Street after the exiled French royal family who stayed at nearby Hartwell from 1807 to 1814.

52. Temple Street probably received its name in honour of the Temple/Grenville family of Stowe who owned property in the town and purchased the manorial rights of Aylesbury in 1802. The street was formerly called Cordwainers' Street or Cobblers' Row.

53. George Street, the road linking Temple Square to Kingsbury, was earlier called Hog Lane. It is seen here during the winter of 1947.

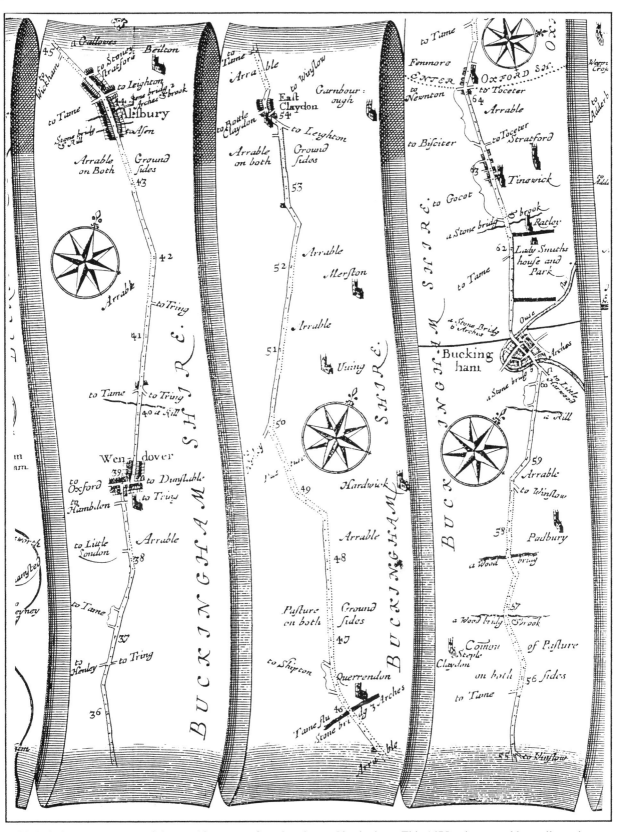

54. Aylesbury was on one of the coaching routes from London to Birmingham. This 1675 strip map told travellers what to expect in the way of bridges, crossroads, distances and even the cultivation of the land either side of the road. North of Aylesbury, the coach road went through Quarrendon and utilised part of a Roman road on its way to Buckingham.

55. When the road through Aylesbury was turnpiked in 1721 by the Buckingham and Wendover Trust, the route to the north was along Buckingham Street towards Whitchurch and Winslow.

56. The turnpike went south along Walton Street where the carriageway was lowered, creating the raised footpath shown in this photograph.

57. The town was eventually encircled by turnpike houses where the toll collectors opened and closed the gates. This elevation of the Walton turnpike dates from 1831.

58. The turnpike house was demolished and the materials sold off when the last Buckingham to Wendover Turnpike Act expired in 1878.

Wendover

AYLESBURY & BUCKINGHAM TURNPIKE TRUST.

TO BUILDERS AND OTHERS.

MESSRS. READER AND SON

Have received instructions from the Trustees to SELL by AUCTION, at the BULL'S HEAD INN, AYLESBURY,

On WEDNESDAY, the 30th of OCTOBER, 1878,
At Three for Four o'Clock in the Afternoon punctually,—The whole of the

MATERIALS OF THE TOLL HOUSES

GATES, and FENCES, at WALTON, BUCKINGHAM ROAD, and HOGSTON.

PARTICULARS.

WALTON TURNPIKE HOUSE, GATES, AND MATERIALS.

	Lot	
£1.1.–	1	The Hut, Toll Board, &c., opposite the Three Pigeons
£1.12.6	2	Sixty feet of Wood Fencing, in the Wendover Road, with the Gate and 86 feet of ditto in the Stoke Road, forming the garden fencing
£2.–.–	3	The 11ft. 6in. Turnpike Gate, with the hanging and shutting posts, lock and key, a piece of Fencing, and the Hand Gate and Posts
£1.15.–	4	The like in Stoke Road
–.17.6	5	The Porch in front of House and the two Toll Boards
£15.–.–	6	The whole of the Brick-work forming the Erection of the Octagon Toll House, Barn, Water Closet, &c.
£7.–.–	7	The whole of the Slates, Gutters, Spouting, and Lead, on the roof of same
£3.5.–	8	The whole of the Roofing, Joists, and Floors of the same
£2.–.–	9	Seven Doors and Frames
£3.–.–	10	Eight Window Sashes, Frames, and inside Shutters
£1.12.6	11	Pump, Lead Pipe, Sink, and Water Fittings and Tap
£1.12.6	12	Two Grates, Copper, Cupboard, and Gas Fittings
	10	

BUCKINGHAM ROAD.

£7.15.–	14	Ninty-six feet of Iron Palisading, including the two Swing Gates, the whole of the Stone Coping and Brick Underwork
£1.10.–	15	The Fencing, 27 feet long, comprising 7 Posts, with 5 stout Iron Bars, and the Swing Gate, 28 feet of Wood Fencing round the Cottage Garden, Posts and Gate, and the Boarded Fence as the back
£2.–.–	16	The 12ft. Turnpike Gate, with the hanging and shutting Posts, Collinge' patent hinges, and the latches and fastening-open posts
£2.2.–	17	The ditto Weigh Bridge Gate adjoining, and 40 feet of Fencing and the foot-stile, comprising 12 Posts and the stout Iron Rails
£2.10.–	18	The Porch, in front of House, 4 Flag Stones and Scraper, and the Toll Boards
£18.–.–	19	The whole of the Erection and Materials forming the Stable, Chaise House (with Loft over), 2 Privies, Wood Barn and Pig Stye, brick-built and slated, being 25ft. long, by 18ft. wide
£2.7.6	20	The Lead Pump and Pipe in yard, Flag Stone, Trap and Drain Pipes as the back door, and the Chiltern Hills Water Fittings and Taps
£1.15.–	21	The Lead Cistern, with Pipe, Tap, and overflow pipe
£1.7.6	22	The Copper, as fixed in the Toll House, the Stone Cistern in ditto, the Oven and Boiler Range, and the two Register Stoves
–.17.6	23	The like in the Cottage
£23.–.–	24	The whole of the Brick Work forming the Erection of the Toll House and Cottage, with the lean-to back houses, 34ft. long and 22ft. wide
£11.–.–	25	The whole of the Slates on the same and the Iron Spouting
£2.10.–	26	The whole of the Rafters, Joists, and Floors to the Toll House and Cottage
£1.15.–	27	Twelve Sash and Lead Lights, with the Window Frames and inside Shutters in ditto
£2.10.–	28	Fourteen Doors and Frames in ditto

HOGSTON TOLL GATE AND HOUSE.

£30.–.–	29	The whole of the Materials of the Toll House, namely, the Bricks, Slates, Ridge Tiles, Gutters and Spouting, Wood-work, Doors and Frames, Sashes, Grates, &c., forming the recently-erected Toll House, Barn, and Water Closet, at Hogston
£2.–.–	30	The Turnpike Gate, two Posts, Foot Gate, two Toll Boards, and the Top, Chain, &c., to the Draw Well
£3.3.–	31	Iron Roll
£155.16.–		

May be Viewed at any time prior to the Sale, and Particulars obtained of Messrs. Tindal and Baynes, Clerks to the Trustees, or of the Auctioneers, Temple Street, Aylesbury.

£156.13.6

DE FRAINE, PRINTER, "BUCKS HERALD" OFFICE, WALTON-STREET, AYLESBURY.

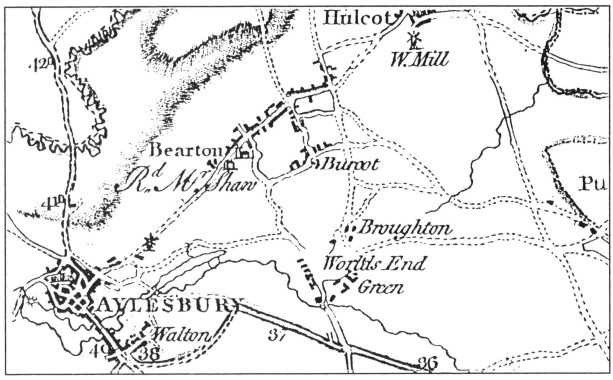

59. The road from Tring was turnpiked in 1762 as the Sparrows Herne to Walton Trust, named after the precise localities where it joined on to other turnpike trusts. Until 1826, the turnpike road ran through the hamlet of Walton as can be seen on Jeffery's map of 1770.

60. The Sparrows Herne turnpike road was diverted in 1826 so as to avoid Walton and to enter Aylesbury by a more direct road called New Road. Only in the 1880s did the road acquire its present name of High Street.

61. New Road was at first a residential area. In this view looking up the street, Tring Villas are still visible behind Longley's drapery store.

62. The building of New Road meant the demolition of several buildings at the north-east corner of the Market Square. The front part of the *Crown Inn* was rebuilt at this time. The inn was completely swept away in 1937 when Market House was built.

63. The Bicester to Aylesbury road was a continuation of the Sparrows Herne to Walton turnpike. The Trust started in 1770. This road was, like the Buckingham road, an important north-south route linking London and Birmingham.

64. The road to Oxford was turnpiked in 1770 as the Aylesbury to Little Milton Trust. It entered Aylesbury via Hartwell and Duck End.

65. The original turnpike collector's house stood here on the Oxford Road corner with White Hill. The taller building is the *Seven Stars* beerhouse, demolished in the 1920s.

66. Cambridge Street was the beginning of the Aylesbury to Hockliffe turnpike, the last of Aylesbury's roads to be turnpiked in 1810. It linked the town to Watling Street just over the county boundary at Hockliffe.

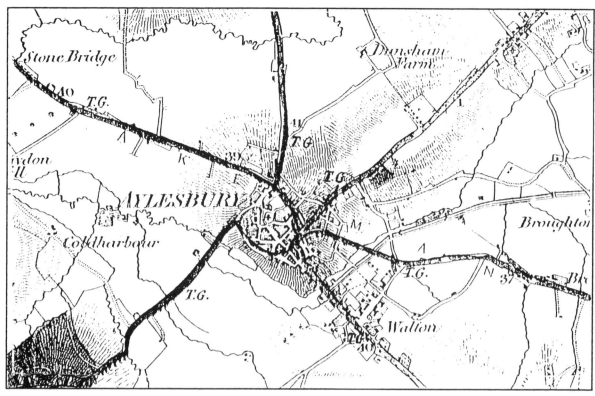

67. The six turnpike gates are marked on this 1834 Ordnance Survey map.

68. The Aylesbury branch of the Grand Junction Canal was opened in 1815. This view shows narrow boats at the wharf next to Walton Mill in 1921.

69. The wharf at Aylesbury about 1900. The Grand Junction Canal was one of the most prosperous in the country. It was a broad canal with locks wide enough for barges. The Buckingham, Aylesbury and Wendover branches were built with cheaper narrow locks putting these towns at something of a disadvantage.

70. Aylesbury can boast the first branch line in the country, being connected to the London to Birmingham Railway at Cheddington as early as 1839. This original station building was at the end of Railway Street but was replaced by a new station on the High Street in 1889.

71. An ex-London Midland & Scottish 2-4-2 tank engine and passenger train at Aylesbury in 1949. This was the slowest route to London and was used mainly for goods traffic.

72. The Wycombe Railway was the next to reach Aylesbury in 1863. As the company was associated with the Great Western Railway, the line was built to the 7ft. gauge but reduced to standard gauge in 1868 when it linked up with the Aylesbury to Buckingham Railway. This view shows an ex-G.W.R. 2-6-2 tank engine at Aylesbury in 1948.

73. With the opening of the Metropolitan Railway line via Amersham and Wendover in 1892, Aylesbury acquired a third route to London. This was used by the Great Central as part of their new line to London from 1899, at last giving Aylesbury main line services north and south. Here two ex-L.N.E.R. 4-6-0 locomotives wait at Aylesbury with a Manchester to London train in 1948.

74. Bus services brought unwelcome competition to the railways. The cheap travel they offered induced many to forsake their local market towns and shop in the larger centres like Aylesbury.

Grand Junction Canal, Aylesbury.

75. Aylesbury's position as a market centre for the Vale would ensure that its two mills were kept busy, as long as there was sufficient water in the Bear Brook to power them. Both added steam power in the 19th century. The narrow boat is loading at Hills & Partridge's Walton mill.

76. Market towns can be expected to have several breweries with tied pubs situated within a days journey by horse and cart. The largest concern was Terry's Walton brewery. It amalgamated with Dell's brewery to form the Aylesbury Brewery Company in the 1890s. Even when taken over by Hall's in 1989, A.B.C. still had 85 tied pubs. The Walton Brewery site is seen here in 1947.

77. The old brewery in Bourbon Street was run by the Dell family. They probably acquired the site through the marriage of Martha Dell to John Delafield, a partner in the company which had supplied water to the neighbourhood from this site in the 18th century. The brewery was demolished in 1894 to make way for the Public Baths.

78. The London printers Hazell & Watson established a branch works at Aylesbury in 1867. These buildings on the corner of Tring Road and Walton Road were commenced in 1879.

79. The printing works of Hazell, Watson & Viney in 1897. By this time the firm employed about 500 people.

80. A similar view of Hazell's taken about 1920 shows the rapid expansion of the business.

81. Aylesbury's condensed milk factory was commenced in 1870. Milk from local farms was brought in daily, its water content evaporated and sugar added. The product was canned on site and shipped by narrow boat along the Grand Junction Canal.

S.G.P.R. 20.3.1912.

82. The Aylesbury photographer S. G. Payne was on hand to record this strange event at the Walton Engine Works, Walton Road, in 1912. The proprietor, William C. Morris, described himself as an iron and brass founder and agricultural and general engineer.

83. The Bifurcated and Tubular Rivet Company built its Aylesbury factory off the Stoke Road in 1910.

84. This early advertisement demonstrates the principle and the simplicity of the bifurcated rivet.

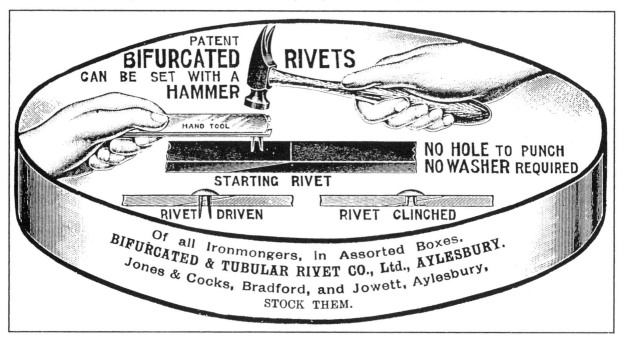

85. Loading aluminium ingots at International Alloys Bicester Road plant. Built in 1940, the factory recycled scrap aluminium and made high quality ingots for conversion into aluminium products. The factory chimneys were a local landmark until closure in 1982 brought about the clearance of the site for Tesco's superstore.

86. Aylesbury came to an agreement with London County Council to take 'overspill' population in 1958. Land was set aside for new factories to provide work for the newcomers. Klockner-Moeller started manufacturing electronic control systems in Aylesbury in 1960 and moved to these purpose-built premises on the Gatehouse industrial estate in 1971.

87. St Mary's church is one of only four Buckinghamshire churches directly mentioned in Domesday Book. Its importance at that time can be judged from the entry for Stoke Mandeville which 'belongs to the church of Aylesbury' and from the reference that each freeman of the eight hundreds around Aylesbury 'having one hide or more renders one load of grain to this church'.

88. St Mary's church was heavily restored in the 1860s under the direction of the Buckinghamshire-born church architect Sir George Gilbert Scott. Note the new east window of three lancets replacing the perpendicular window shown in the previous illustration.

89. The interior of St Mary's church looking through the chancel arch towards Scott's early-English east window.

90. The interior of St Mary's church looking towards the perpendicular west window. The seating shown here was installed in the 1850s, replacing box pews, many of which had been jealously guarded as the property of individual local families. The Victorian benches meant to seat 1,150 have themselves now been removed and more flexible seating provided.

91. Rapidly expanding populations caused the churches to provide more capacity in Victorian towns. Aylesbury gained Holy Trinity church, Walton, in 1843 providing another 600 seats.

92. St John's church was an attempt to provide accommodation for the expanding east of Aylesbury. Built in 1883, fronting Cambridge Street, it was entirely brick-built and somewhat utilitarian, but it provided 600 seats. A chancel was added in 1895, but the whole was demolished in 1970.

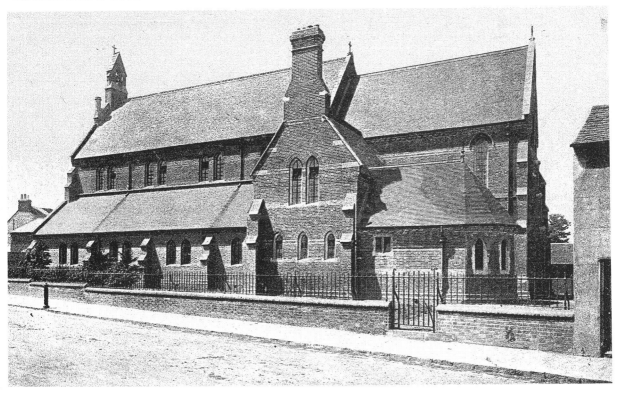

93. A presbyterian congregation began to meet here at Hale Leys in 1707. Their place of worship was taken over in 1816 by the congregationalists who built this new church on the site in 1874 to seat 650. When the Hale Leys shopping centre was built in the 1970s, only the tower was retained.

94. The congregationalists had originally met at this site in Castle Street. The classical façade on the left was a 19th-century addition and the earlier chapel and burial ground, dating back to 1788, must have been behind the line of houses. The chapel was used for many years as a Sunday school connected with Hale Leys. It was demolished in 1981.

95. The Friends' Meeting House in Rickford's Hill was built in 1727 in the garden of a house formerly licensed for worship. It is still in use.

96. Another meeting house in a secluded position was that of the Baptists in Cambridge Street built in 1733. It was vacated by them in 1828, when a handsome new chapel to seat 200 was built on Walton Street. The old meeting house was demolished in 1938, the new chapel followed in 1966.

St. Joseph's, Aylesbury

97. 'Iron rooms' were a popular solution to growing church numbers. The Roman Catholics put up this one in the High Street in 1892. It was replaced by the present St Joseph's church in 1935.

98. The original Wesleyan chapel in Friarage Path was built in 1837. Superseded by the Buckingham Street chapel in 1894, it continued as a Sunday school until sold to the Comrades Club in 1919. It was demolished to make way for the Friar's Square shopping centre.

99. The most elaborate of the non-conformist places of worship, the Wesleyan chapel in Buckingham Street, was built in 1894 to seat 650.

100. Aylesbury's Free Grammar School (the building on the right next to the churchyard) was founded by Sir Henry Lee of Quarrendon in the late 16th century. The bequest of £5,000 in the will of Henry Phillips, a native of Aylesbury who died in London in 1714, provided for a new school and master's house, built in 1719. The building ceased to be a school in 1907 and is now part of the County Museum.

101. St Mary's school was built in 1845 as a National School, promoted by the 'National Society for the Education of the Poor in the Principles of the Established Church'. It had space for 360 children. The schools attached to St John's church and to Holy Trinity, Walton, also began as National Schools. St John's in Cambridge Street was the largest with 430 places; Holy Trinity could accommodate 230.

102. The British School in Pebble Lane, promoted by the British and Foreign Schools Society, was built on land purchased on the sale of the former workhouse in 1830. Rebuilt in 1872 and enlarged in 1885, it provided places for 556 children of non-conformist families. When it closed in 1907, the children were moved to Queen's Park school. The building became the Education Sub-office and was for many years the home of the County Library Service.

103. Queen's Park County School was the first in Aylesbury built by the County Council under powers given them by the 1902 Education Act. It had places for 390 boys, 350 girls and 310 infants, educating them from the age of five up to fourteen.

104. Another view of Queen's Park School, this one from the 1950s.

105. Under the 1902 Act, the County Council was able to help the old endowed grammar schools to build new premises and to offer scholarships to those who passed an examination. The new Grammar School in Walton Road was built in 1906-7 to accommodate 150 children. After the building of a new wing in 1931 the school had places for 350 boys and girls, of which about 40 were scholarship places.

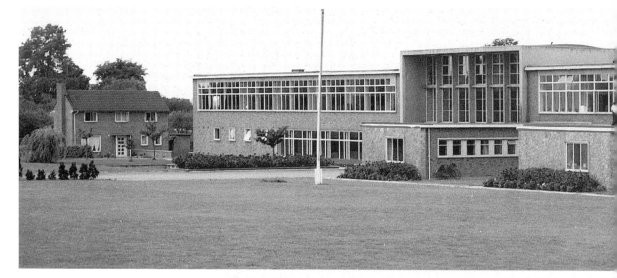

106. Billed as the biggest school building project since before the war, Grange School was built as a secondary modern school under the 1944 Education Act. It had places for 600 pupils and opened in 1954.

107. Until 1834 each parish was responsible for its own poor and the larger villages and towns provided parish workhouses for their accommodation. Aylesbury's parish workhouse stood on the corner of Pebble Lane and the churchyard. It still stands and can be seen on this view just beyond the old Grammar School.

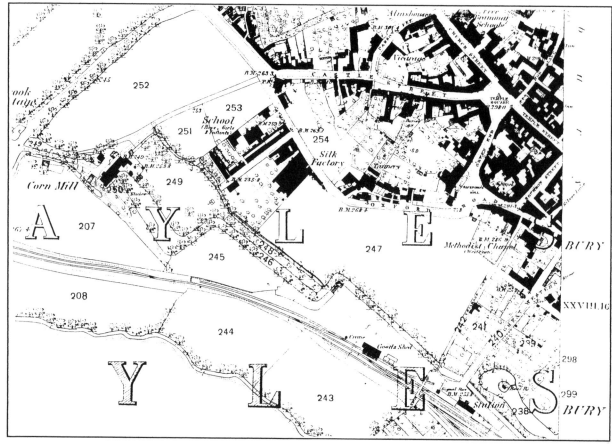

108. Agricultural change had brought about large-scale unemployment by the 1820s. Aylesbury's workhouse was overflowing and a new building was erected between Oxford Road and the corn mill in 1829. It was soon to be superseded by the Union Workhouse on Bierton Road but its site is marked on the early Ordnance Survey maps by a silk mill, originally put up to find work for the inmates.

109. The Poor Law Act of 1834 created unions of parishes based on large towns like Aylesbury. The poor from all the neighbouring villages were accommodated in the new Union Workhouse built in Bierton Road in 1844.

110. The County Gaol was built opposite the Workhouse in 1845 and provided individual cells for the 250 prisoners. The silence rule was applied and the prison chapel had 274 seats so arranged that the prisoners could all see the clergyman but could not see each other. By the time the photograph was taken the gaol had become a Female Convict Prison. It is now a Young Offenders Institution.

111. In 1832 a group of the local gentry led by Dr. Lee of Hartwell formed a committee to start an infirmary. They purchased a large house on the corner of the Bicester and Buckingham Roads and fitted it out as a hospital the following year. The present Royal Bucks Hospital (now empty) was erected in 1861-2 behind the original building which was then demolished.

Royal Bucks Hospital.

112. The influence of Florence Nightingale on the design of the new hospital can be seen in this view of one of the principal wards. It was spacious and airy, measuring 81ft. by 25ft. with the ceiling 16ft. high. Florence Nightingale was the sister-in-law of Sir Harry Verney, then president of the management committee.

113. The County Hall dates from the 1720s. It originally had three entrances; the one on the east led to the gaol and is now blocked, the central door gave access to the office of the Clerk of the Peace, and the west door was for the courts. Following the Local Government Act of 1888, the new Buckinghamshire County Council based itself here.

114. By the 1920s the various County Council officials were dispersed around several buildings in the town. New County Offices were built on the site of these houses in Walton Street in 1928-9.

115. Lord Cottesloe laying the foundation stone of the new County Offices in September 1928.

116. The New County Offices, Walton Street, with cast iron railings which were removed during the war.

117. The county administration continued to expand, leading to the building of the New County Hall in 1966. It included a new library headquarters for the county. The library can be seen here under construction with the older offices and the cattle market in the background.

List of Members and Officers.

Mr. P. Davis *(Sanitary Inspector)*	**Mr. P. A. Wright** *(Clerk)*	**Dr. T. G. Parrott** *(Medical Officer)*	**Mr. J. T. Broderick**	**Mr. C. C. Chilton**	**Mr. C. F. Adkins**
Mr. J. S. Mayne *(Rate Collector)*	**Mr. W. J. Cook**	**Mr. W. H. Taylor** *(Surveyor)*	**Mr. G. J. Thrasher**	**Mr. G. Putman**	**Mr. T. Sherriff**
		Mr. J. Turner	**Mr. E. R. Franklin**	**Mr. H. L. Nippin**	**Mr. W. Smith**
Mr. T. Green	**Mr. J. C. Garner**		**Mr. J. Reader**	**Mr. R. J. Elliston**	**Mr. W. H. Gilkes**

118. Aylesbury's own affairs were run from 1849 by a Board of Health which set about providing adequate sewerage and other necessities of a growing town. In 1894, the board was replaced by an Urban District Council seen here in 1908. After a long campaign by the U.D.C., Aylesbury's status was changed to Municipal Borough whose council served the town until reorganisation in 1974.

119. A useful addition to Aylesbury's facilities was the Public Baths, built on the site of Dell's Brewery in 1895 with a large proportion of the cost met by the Rothschilds of Waddesdon. The swimming bath measured 62ft. by 21ft. The building was demolished to make way for Friar's Square shopping centre.

120. The site of the Vale Park was purchased by the Borough Council in 1929. Tennis courts and a putting green were immediately laid out, but the landscaping was not completed until 1937.

121. The Vale Pool was opened in 1935 and is still in use in the summer months.

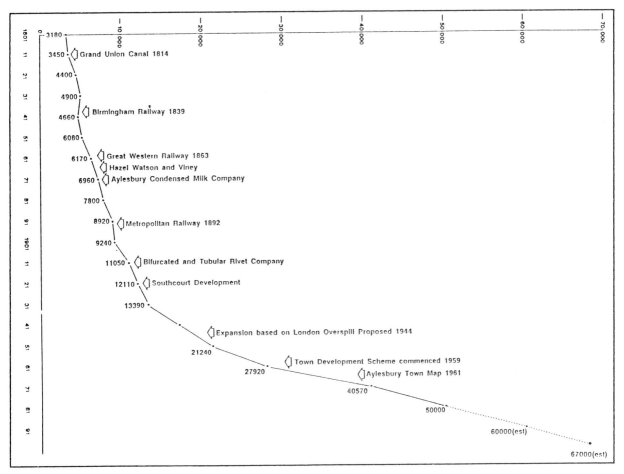

Graph axis labels (top, population): 10,000 · 20,000 · 30,000 · 40,000 · 50,000 · 60,000 · 70,000

Left axis (years): 1801, 11, 21, 31, 41, 51, 61, 71, 81, 91, 1901, 11, 21, 31, 41, 51, 61, 71, 81, 91

Data points and labels:

- 3180
- 3450 — Grand Union Canal 1814
- 4400
- 4900
- 4660 — Birmingham Railway 1839
- 6080
- 6170 — Great Western Railway 1863
- Hazel Watson and Viney
- 6960 — Aylesbury Condensed Milk Company
- 7800
- 8920 — Metropolitan Railway 1892
- 9240
- 11050 — Bifurcated and Tubular Rivet Company
- 12110 — Southcourt Development
- 13390
- Expansion based on London Overspill Proposed 1944
- 21240
- Town Development Scheme commenced 1959
- 27920
- Aylesbury Town Map 1961
- 40570
- 50000
- 60000(est)
- 67000(est)

122. Aylesbury's growth since 1801 is shown by this graph. Population increase was modest by national standards but since the 1930s, the rate of increase has quickened. When Aylesbury adopted the 1952 Town Development Act its population was about 21,000. Under its expansion plan in co-operation with London County Council it was to more than double.

123. Solid Victorian houses were built along most of the main roads out of Aylesbury. These are on High Street near to the canal bridge.

124. Further along High Street, opposite the Condensed Milk Factory, the area known as Queen's Park was developed at the turn of the century.

125. These substantial villas fronting the Wendover Road were built in the 1880s. The repetition of the builders' advertisements in local papers suggests that they were difficult to sell.

126. Victoria Park, north of the Tring Road, was developed in the 1880s. The houses seen here on the left of Victoria Street were however built by Hazell's for their own employees in the 1950s.

127. The expansion of Aylesbury along Bierton Road was a little later. These houses on Bierton Hill were not built until after 1900. The area was known as Manor Park.

128. The Southcourt housing estate was commenced by the Borough Council in 1920. These houses in Moore Avenue, Southcourt were built in the 1930s.

129. These prosperous semi-detached houses were built along Tring Road between the wars, creating the ribbon development so scorned by early town planners.

130. Stonehaven Road, off the Bicester Road, was a more adventurous private housing development of the 1930s.

131. Private housing in Westmorland Avenue, Bedgrove. Bedgrove Farm was purchased by the Borough Council and the whole area, formerly in the parish of Weston Turville, added to the Borough of Aylesbury in 1958.